Cycle with Perseverance

The Story of Jenny Graham's Record-Breaking Journey Around the World

Top Hand Publisher

Table of Contents

INTRODUCTION...**4**

CHAPTER ONE...**7**

    THE BEGINNING.. 7

CHAPTER TWO..**17**

    THE PREPARATION... 17

CHAPTER THREE...**28**

    THE DEPARTURE...28

CHAPTER FOUR...**35**

    THE JOURNEY... 35

CHAPTER FIVE...**50**

    THE RETURN...50

CONCLUSION..**54**

    THE LESSONS...54

INTRODUCTION

Imagine riding a bicycle alone and unsupported across the globe. Imagine traveling more than 18,000 kilometers on your bicycle through 16 nations and four continents. Imagine being alone and having to deal with bad weather, difficult terrain, dangerous animals, technical troubles, and health concerns. Imagine doing this in less than five months while also setting a world record.

It's not a dream, either. This is the motivational tale of Scottish cyclist Jenny Graham, who in 2018 set a record for the quickest female round of the globe without assistance.

Jenny Graham is neither a famous person nor a professional athlete. She is a typical lady with a remarkable enthusiasm for riding and exploration. She is a friend, a sister, a mother, and a daughter. She is also a leader, a pioneer, and a role model.

You may follow Jenny's journey in this book, from her modest beginnings in Scotland to her victorious return to Berlin. You may read about her inspiration, struggles, and triumphs throughout her incredible journey. You will also learn about her tenacity, bravery, and resilience as she conquered her concerns, doubts, and challenges.

You will see how Jenny used her bike to take in the beauty and variety of the globe. You will get to know the individuals she met along the road who inspired her, assisted her, and ended up becoming friends. You'll witness how Jenny encouraged others to pursue their goals and push themselves as well.

This book is more than just a record of Jenny's incredible achievement. The strength of the human spirit and the pleasure of riding is also shown by this. You'll feel emotions while you read this book, including joy, laughter, and awe.

You will be inspired by this book to go after your ambitions and interests.

This book is for everyone, whether you ride a bike or not, whether you're a woman or not, and whether you're young or elderly. It is a book that will demonstrate to you that, with enough persistence, everything is achievable.

CHAPTER ONE

THE BEGINNING

On April 10, 1980, Jenny Graham was born in Inverness, Scotland. She had two brothers and a sister, making her the youngest of four children. Both of her parents were educators who loved the outdoors and the natural world. They often took their kids camping, hiking, and cycling adventures throughout Scotland and beyond.

Jenny received curiosity and a sense of adventure from her parents. She likes to travel and experiment with new things. She also loved playing with her brothers and their friends since she was a tomboy. She didn't mind being filthy, hurt, or confronted.

When Jenny was six years old, her parents gave her a red BMX bike as a birthday gift. She fell in love with it right away and started riding it everywhere. She self-taught herself how to balance, steer, stop, and pedal. She also learned how to repair it when it was damaged or broke down.

Jenny's bike became her closest companion and means of escape. She used it for transportation to school, to see her friends, for doing errands, and for enjoyment. Also, she utilized it as an escape from the difficulties and demands of growing up. Riding her bike, enjoying the breeze in her hair and the sun on her face, gave her comfort and delight.

As Jenny got older, her love for riding developed as well. She began to increase the length and pace of her rides. She joined a neighborhood bicycle club and took part in competitions. She also read cycling-related books and periodicals where she discovered the many bike models, accessories, routes, and methods.

Jenny had a lifelong desire to travel the globe by bicycle. She was motivated by the accounts of well-known riders who had accomplished it in the past, like Mark Beaumont, Dervla Murphy, and Annie Londonderry. She was inspired by their bravery, tenacity, and resolve. She wanted to travel the globe on her bike and continue in their footsteps.

Jenny's ideal, nonetheless, was not simple to realize. Along the journey, she encountered several difficulties and hurdles. She had to strike a balance between her riding interests and her obligations to her family, job, and schooling. She had to cope with the preconceptions and misconceptions that female cyclists had to contend with in a sport that was dominated by males. She had to go over her limits, uncertainties, and concerns.

Jenny persisted in pursuing her goal. She put forth a lot of effort, creating plans, and saving money. She also got help and inspiration from other individuals who loved riding and exploring new places. Former professional mountain cyclist Lee Craigie, who established the Adventure Syndicate in 2016, was one of them.

A group of female cyclists known as The Adventure Syndicate works to encourage and enlist others in the sport of cycling. Women of all ages and abilities, plan events, seminars, rides, and trips. With their website, social media accounts, and podcasts, they also offer their experiences, suggestions, and counsel.

During one of the 2017 Adventure Syndicate events, Jenny and Lee became friends. They hit it off right away and became close. Lee saw Jenny's talent and excitement for riding alone and without backup throughout the globe. She volunteered to be Jenny's mentor and guide her through the task.

Jenny happily accepted Lee's offer. She became a volunteer and a member of the Adventure Syndicate. Lee and the other ladies in the group taught her a lot, as did she. She learned from them how to map out her journey, choose her gear, handle her finances and logistics, prepare emotionally and physically for challenges, deal with setbacks, and deal with loneliness.

Becoming a member of the Adventure Syndicate gave Jenny more self-assurance and drive. She realized that she was not alone in her fight or her desire. She saw that many other ladies were riding their bikes and doing remarkable things. She was moved by their testimonies and accomplishments.

In 2018, Jenny decided to take on the challenge of riding alone and without assistance across the globe. She chose June 16, 2018, as her departure date from Berlin, Germany. She decided on Berlin since it was the starting point of Mark Beaumont's record-breaking ride in 2017.

Jenny wanted to finish her journey faster than Paola Gianotti's record-breaking time of 144 days, which she established in 2014. Jenny was aware that her aim was lofty, but she had faith that if she pedaled steadily and persistently, she could achieve it.

Jenny posted about her strategy to her social media followers, close friends, and family. They reacted to her in different ways. Others were happy for her and supportive. Several expressed skepticism and safety concerns for her. Her aim was met with indifference or dismissal by others.

Jenny was grateful for the encouragement but disregarded the criticism. She was confident in her ability to overcome the task, her thorough preparation, and her dedication to riding. She was prepared to go off on her once-in-a-lifetime journey.

Jenny prepared for her travel by putting everything she would need on her bike and in her luggage. She rode a custom steel cycle with belt drive, a Rohloff hub, and 29-inch wheels. She carried a handlebar bag, a frame bag, and four panniers. She had a solar panel, a stove, a water filter, a tent, and a sleeping bag. She had money, clothing, equipment, extra parts, maps, and paperwork. She also carried a laptop, a smartphone, a camera, and a satellite tracker.

The combined weight of Jenny's bike and baggage was roughly 55 kg. They had to be transported on her bike by her alone. She lacked a squad or backup vehicle to assist her. To finish her journey, she had to depend entirely on her power, abilities, and materials.

Before leaving for Berlin, Jenny bid farewell to her friends and family in Scotland. Lachlan, her son who was 19 years old at the time, was with her. Jenny's sole kid and staunchest ally was Lachlan. He was elated by his mother's ambition. He also enjoyed adventure and riding, much like her.

On June 15, 2018, Jenny and Lachlan landed in Berlin. They remained at a hostel close to Jenny's starting point for her ride the next day, which was the Brandenburg Gate. While eating pizza and watching movies, they spent the evening inspecting Jenny's bike and belongings.

The next morning, Jenny got up early and prepared for her trip. She put on her helmet, sunglasses, and riding gear. She boarded a cab, loaded her luggage and bike, and drove to the Brandenburg Gate. She felt both anxious and eager.

By 9:30 a.m., she arrived at the Brandenburg Gate. Lee Craigie and a few other Adventure Syndicate members who had come to see her depart met her. They hugged her, kissed her, and encouraged her. They also assisted her with setting up her baggage and bike.

Jenny double-checked the functionality of her smartphone and satellite tracker. She looked at her watch to see the time as well. That was nine-thirty. She was prepared to go.

She hopped on her bicycle and grinned at the camera capturing her departure. Lee and the others who were supporting her waved back at her. She inhaled deeply and began cycling.

She exited via the Brandenburg Gate and moved toward Poland in the east. When she arrived back in Berlin, she still had 18,000 kilometers to go. She had no clue what obstacles she would face. She was just certain that she would cycle steadily.

CHAPTER TWO

THE PREPARATION

The commencement of Jenny's global voyage did not occur on June 16, 2018. Long before that, she decided to accept the challenge and started getting ready for it. Jenny's planning focused on four key areas: the route, the tools, the spending plan, and logistics.

Route

The Guinness World Records for solo, unsupported cycling around the globe served as the basis for Jenny's path. These instructions required Jenny to:

- Begin and end in the same location.
- Move only in one way
At least two antipodal points (points on opposing sides of the earth) must be crossed, as

well as a minimum of 18,000 miles and four continents.
- Travel to at least 16 nations

Jenny decided to ride along Mark Beaumont's path, who in 2017 broke the record for the fastest man cyclist. She intended to repeatedly:

- Europe: Finland, Latvia, Lithuania, Latvia, Germany, Poland
- Asia: South Korea, China, Mongolia, and Kazakhstan
- Australia: Brisbane to Perth
North and South Islands of New Zealand
- North America: from Halifax to Anchorage
Argentina, Chile, and Peru are all in South America.

Jenny's antipodal points were close to Wellington, New Zealand, and Madrid, Spain. She calculated the entire distance traveled along her journey to be about 18,500 miles.

Jenny thoroughly investigated her route utilizing books, maps, and other resources. Also, she sought advice from other cyclists who had completed similar journeys or who resided in the nations she planned to visit. She gained knowledge of each location's topography, climate, culture, language, laws, and traditions. She also pointed us to the finest routes to take, along with the greatest locations to eat, stay, and relax.

She didn't map out her journey carefully or adhere to a set timetable. She likes to have some spontaneity and freedom on her travels. Along the process, she also wanted to allow some space for unexpected events and discoveries. She didn't know exactly where she was going or how long it would take her.

Equipment

The only things Jenny had were her bike and her luggage. These would be her primary traveling companions and tools, so she had to choose them wisely.

Custom-made steel wheels, a Rohloff hub, and a belt drive were features of Jenny's bicycle. She chose this bike because it was dependable, long-lasting, and simple to care for. She also admired its sleek and understated design.

The qualities of Jenny's bike made it appropriate for her journey. It had:

- A Brooks seat that was cozy and long-lasting - A dynamo hub that produced energy from her pedaling and powered her lights and gadgets - A Jones H-bar that enabled different hand positions and comfort -
- A Tubus back rack held her panniers; - A Sonder front rack held her tent and sleeping bag; - A Revelate frame bag had her tools and spare parts; - A Revelate handlebar bag held her maps, paperwork, and snacks.

Without her baggage, Jenny's bike weighed roughly 15 pounds. In honor of one of her favorite artists, Stevie Nicks, she gave it the name "Stevie."

Everything Jenny needed for her trip was in her suitcases. She had a handlebar bag, a frame bag, two front panniers, and two rear panniers. While she wasn't riding her bike, she also had a rucksack that she carried on her back.

Jenny's luggage included:

- A sleeping bag, sleeping pad, pillow, and tent
- A water filter, a burner, a saucepan, a cup, and a spoon.
- Clothing appropriate for various climates (including cycling clothes, casual clothes, underwear, socks, shoes, gloves, hat, and sunglasses)
- Her bike's spare parts and tools (including a pump, a multitool, a chain tool, a spoke wrench, a tire lever, a patch kit, a spare tube, a spare tire,

a spare belt, a spare brake pad, and a spare cable)

- Maps, papers, and cash (including a passport, a visa, an ID card, a credit card, a debit card, some cash in different currencies, and some emergency contacts)
- Accessories and devices (including a satellite tracker, a smartphone, a camera, a laptop, a solar panel, a power bank, some chargers, and some cables)
- Toiletries and personal things (including a toothbrush, toothpaste, soap, shampoo, a towel, sunscreen, a lip balm, deodorant, a comb, a razor, and some sanitary pads)
- Water and food (including some dried fruits, nuts, bars, biscuits, and chocolate for snacks; some rice, pasta, noodles, and soup for meals; and some water bottles and bladders for hydration)

The combined weight of Jenny's suitcases was roughly 40 kg. They had to be transported on her bike by her alone. To maximize the available space and evenly distribute the weight, she had to pack them tightly and effectively. Also, she had to frequently inspect them to make sure they were safe and unbroken.

Budget

Jenny's spending plan was based on her anticipated trip costs. She had to think about the expenses of:

- Flights: At the beginning of her journey, she had to travel from Scotland to Berlin, and after her tour, she had to fly from Berlin to Scotland. Along the way, she had to fly through various continents (such as from South Korea to Australia and from New Zealand to North America).
- Lodging: She liked to tent whenever she could to save money and take in the scenery. Yet sometimes, for her safety or comfort, she had to stay in motels or hostels (such as in big cities or in bad weather conditions).
- Food: She often used her stove and saucepan to prepare her meals. She did, however, sometimes

eat out for convenience or other reasons (such as in restaurants or street stalls).

- Mode of transportation: She spent most of her time cycling. She did, however, sometimes travel by other means when it was necessary or more practical to do so (such as trains or buses).

- Visas: She had to get visas before traveling to several countries (such as Russia or China). She had to pay the fees and apply for them in advance.

- Insurance: In case of accidents or thefts, she wanted insurance for both herself and her bike. Before leaving, she had to purchase it, and she had to renew it monthly.

Jenny spent almost a year getting ready for her adventure. She devoted numerous days and hours to planning, practicing, and testing. She also put a lot of effort and passion into psyching herself up for the task. She had to confront her worries, uncertainties, and concerns. She also had to cope with other people's expectations, viewpoints, and responses.

Jenny's preparation was everything from simple or uncomplicated. Along the journey, she encountered several obstacles and failures. She had to overcome a few technical challenges, like obtaining the proper visa or locating the appropriate bike. She also had to deal with certain personal challenges, such as juggling her obligations to her family and job or handling stress and pressure.

Despite these obstacles and failures, Jenny persisted. She patiently and persistently addressed each problem one at a time. When she needed it, she also asked others for assistance and support. She developed her abilities and understanding by reflecting on her errors. Both as a person and a rider, she developed.

The planning Jenny did was very fruitful and entertaining. Along the road, she encountered several enjoyable and enduring moments. She made a lot of intriguing and motivating friends and learned a lot from them. Also, she traveled to a lot of breathtaking locations, which enriched and awed her.

The planning that Jenny did was crucial to her trip. It served as both a means and an aim in and of itself. It was an adventure inside an adventure, a challenge within a challenge, and a trip within a journey.

Jenny was prepared for her trip across the globe thanks to her planning.

CHAPTER THREE

THE DEPARTURE

On June 16, 2018, Jenny left Berlin, marking the conclusion of her planning and the start of her voyage. That was an exciting, uneasy, and determined time. It was a time for goodbye, thanks, and optimism. That was a historic, difficult, and adventurous time.

By 9:30 am, Jenny arrived at the Brandenburg Gate. Lee Craigie and a few other Adventure Syndicate members who had come to see her depart met her. They hugged her, kissed her, and encouraged her. They also assisted her with setting up her baggage and bike.

Jenny double-checked the functionality of her smartphone and satellite tracker. She looked at her watch to see the time as well. That was nine-thirty. She was prepared to go.

She hopped on her bicycle and grinned at the camera capturing her departure. Lee and the others who were supporting her waved back at her. She inhaled deeply and began cycling.

She exited via the Brandenburg Gate and moved toward Poland in the east. When she arrived back in Berlin, she still had 18,000 kilometers to go. She had no clue what obstacles she would face. She was just certain that she would cycle steadily.

When Jenny departed Berlin, she experienced a range of feelings. She was pleased with herself and proud of taking up the task. She regretted leaving her friends and family behind and experienced sadness. She was intrigued and anxious to explore the world on her bike. Concerned about the challenges and hazards she could encounter, she experienced fear and anxiety.

Jenny made an effort to concentrate on the advantages of her travel. She reminded herself of her motivations and objectives. She also recalled the encouragement and motivation she had gotten from others. She assured herself that she was not the only one going through what she was.

Jenny made an effort to take pleasure in the current stage of her adventure. She was impressed by Berlin's landscape and architecture. She paid attention to the languages and noises of the city. She scented the street's cuisine and flowers. She experienced the sun and breeze on her skin.

Jenny rode her bike towards the countryside after leaving Berlin. She rode beside a riverside bike path. She went through several fields, woods, and settlements. She saw several birds, animals, and flowers. She said hello to a few folks, bikers, and pedestrians.

One day, Jenny cycled for almost six hours. She traveled a total of roughly 80 miles. Every hour or so, she would pause to relax, eat, drink, or consult her map. She would periodically pause to update her blog or social media, snap a few pictures, or record a video.

At about 4 o'clock, Jenny arrived in Frankfurt an der Oder. It was a town on the border between Poland and Germany. She would spend her first night of the voyage there.

Jenny located a campground close to the river. She made a little payment there to set up her tent. She also took a shower, washed her clothes, and charged her gadgets at their facilities. She also purchased some from a neighboring store of some food and drink.

Jenny unpacked her belongings and erected her tent. On the stove, she prepared some spaghetti and soup, which she served with some bread and cheese. She further drank some tea and water. She had been riding all day and was now hungry and thirsty.

Jenny looked at her smartphone and satellite tracker to see how far and how quickly she had traveled. To see whether she received any messages or remarks from others, she also checked her email and social media accounts. She was happy to find that her friends, family, and supporters had given her some encouraging words and comments.

Jenny detailed her first day of travel in a blog post. She spoke about leaving Berlin, her journey, her pauses, her sights, and her emotions. Also, she posted some of the pictures and videos she had shot while traveling. She hoped that people who were interested in her experience would learn from and be inspired by her blog.

Using her smartphone, Jenny made a call to her son Lachlan. She enquired about his well-being and current activities. She also discussed her day and her feelings with him. He received her gratitude for his love and support. She also wished him a nice night and a happy tomorrow.

After squeezing herself into her sleeping bag, Jenny shut her eyes. She was thrilled but also exhausted. She felt both humble and proud. She was elated yet at ease. She had a good feeling about tomorrow.

She slept off while listening to the adjacent river flow.

CHAPTER FOUR

THE JOURNEY

The centerpiece of Jenny's book and the primary component of her challenge was her travels throughout the globe. 18,000 miles were traveled in 16 different nations and on four different continents. It took 124 days, 10 hours, and 50 minutes to complete the trek. That was an exciting, difficult, and educational trip.

Each segment of Jenny's tour, which was broken up into numerous parts, focused on a particular continent or geographic area that she cycled through. Each portion has its traits, difficulties, and pleasures. Likewise, each part has its history, inhabitants, and customs.

We shall succinctly review each phase of Jenny's journey in this chapter. We'll also focus on some of the most notable and memorable experiences she had along the road.

Europe

By cycling across Germany, Poland, Latvia, Lithuania, Russia, and Finland, Jenny began her voyage through Europe. In this phase, she traveled around 2,000 miles in about two weeks.

The following were some of this section's highlights:

- Passing through Berlin's Brandenburg Gate, where she began and ended her trek.
- Cycling along the Baltic Sea shore, taking in the view and the wind; - traveling to Lithuania to the Hill of Crosses, where she observed tens of thousands of crosses built by pilgrims.
- Cycling across the Trans-Siberian Highway, where she encountered high traffic, bumpy roads, and wild dogs. - Crossing the border into Russia, where she had to cope with a drawn-out and difficult visa application procedure.
- Arriving in St. Petersburg, where she was impressed by the city's architecture and history

- Boarding a ship from St. Petersburg to Helsinki, where she made friends with several welcoming other passengers

These were a few of the difficulties in this section:

- Overcoming the language barrier, particularly in Russia where not many people knew English;
- Adjusting to the heat and humidity, which caused her to perspire and get dehydrated
- Locating affordable or adequate camping or lodging options - Avoiding the many and bothersome mosquitoes and ticks

Asia

Jenny resumed her tour throughout Asia, cycling through South Korea, Kazakhstan, China, and Mongolia. In this phase, she traveled around 6,000 miles in about six weeks.

The following were some of this section's highlights:

- Traveling from Azerbaijan to Kazakhstan by boat over the Caspian Sea, where she witnessed dolphins and sunsets
- Entering China at the Khorgos border crossing, where she saw a stark difference between the two countries; - Riding over the Kazakh desert, where she felt immensity and loneliness
- She rode a bicycle down the Silk Road, an old trading route
- Traveling to Xi'an where she had great meals and visited the Terracotta Army
- Crossing the Gobi Desert in Mongolia through sandstorms and heat waves.

Upon arriving in Ulaanbaatar, she celebrated her birthday and made friends with other cyclists. She then flew to Seoul, where she changed her bike and gear. She then cycled through South Korea, taking in both the contemporary and traditional features of the nation. Finally, she finished her Asian leg in Osaka.

These were a few of the difficulties in this section:

- Handling immigration complications, particularly in China where she had to submit numerous visa applications and abide by rigorous regulations.
- Handling the traffic and pollution, particularly in China, where she was confronted with massive cities, busy highways, and smoggy air
- Locating appropriate campsites or lodging, particularly in Mongolia, where she had to contend with nomads, dogs, and wolves.
- Preventing food poisoning, particularly in China when she consumed some dubious food and was ill

Australia

In Australia, Jenny continued her adventure by cycling from Perth to Brisbane. In this phase, she traveled around 3,000 miles in about three weeks.

The following were some of this section's highlights:

- Cycling through the cliffs and beaches of the Indian Ocean, where she saw breathtaking sunsets;
- Crossing the Nullarbor Plain, where she was struck by its isolation and scope.
- Traveling to Adelaide, where she made some new friends among the locals and cyclists.
- As she rode a bicycle through the Great Dividing Range, she encountered some hills and forests.
- Arrived in Brisbane, where she met some friends and marked the halfway point.

These were a few of the difficulties in this section:

- Managing the heat and dryness, which caused her to perspire and get dehydrated
- Locating acceptable campsites or accommodations was difficult or costly.

- Avoiding snakes and spiders, which were dangerous and deadly, was a challenge. She also had to contend with headwinds and crosswinds, which slowed her down and left her fatigued.

New Zealand

In New Zealand, Jenny resumed her tour by cycling both the North and South Islands. During this phase, she traveled around 1,500 miles in two weeks.

The following were some of this section's highlights:

She saw gorgeous bays, islands, and lighthouses while riding along the Pacific Ocean coast.
- On a ferry across the Cook Strait, where she spotted dolphins and whales
- Traveling to Christchurch, where she saw the city's strength and rehabilitation after the earthquake;

- Cycling through the Southern Alps, where she marveled at the mountains, lakes, glaciers, and volcanoes
- Arrived in Wellington, where she saw several friends and crossed one of her antipodal points.

These were a few of the difficulties in this section:

She struggled to ascend and move quickly because of the hills and headwinds. She also shivered and soaked because of the chilly and rainy conditions.

Locating affordable or acceptable camping or lodging was a challenge, as were autos and trucks, which were hazardous and moved quickly.

The Americas

In North America, Jenny continued her quest by cycling from Alaska to Halifax. In this phase, she traveled around 5,000 miles in about five weeks.

The following were some of this section's highlights:

- Traveling the Alaska Highway, where she witnessed breathtaking mountains, glaciers, and animals; - Entering Canada, where she was greeted with a smile and handed a passport stamp;
- When bicycling across the Rocky Rockies, she encountered some difficult ascents and descents. When cycling across the Great Plains, she encountered immensity and loneliness. When she arrived in Toronto, she celebrated her birthday and ran with some friends. While cycling down the St. Lawrence River, she took in the landscape and the history.
- Arrived in Halifax, where she completed her journey across North America.

These were a few of the difficulties in this section:

- Finding suitable places to camp or stay, which were hard to come by or expensive - Dealing with the bears and moose, which were curious and unpredictable.
- Handling the heat and humidity, which caused her to perspire and become dehydrated.
- Avoiding mosquitoes and flies, which were numerous and inconvenient.

Latin America

In South America, Jenny resumed her adventure on the bicycle, passing through Chile, Peru, and Argentina. In this phase, she traveled around 2,000 miles in about two weeks.

The following were some of this section's highlights:

- She witnessed stunning beaches, cliffs, and sunsets while riding along the Pacific Ocean coast.

- Traveling through the Andes Mountains, where she marveled at the mountains, lakes, and volcanoes - Stopping at Cusco to see the Inca culture and ruins
- Reaching Buenos Aires, where she passed her second antipodal point and visited several friends, she suffered the Atacama Desert's heat and dryness.

These were a few of the difficulties in this section:

- Finding suitable places to camp or stay, especially in Argentina where she had to contend with police, locals, and dogs. Coping with the altitude and thin air, made her breathe quickly and feel lightheaded. Coping with the traffic and pollution, especially in Peru where she encountered chaotic cities, busy roads, and smoggy air.
- Preventing food poisoning, particularly after eating some dubious food in Peru and being ill

Europe

In Europe, where she rode through Portugal, Spain, France, Holland, and Germany, Jenny came to an end on her voyage. In this phase, she traveled around 2,000 miles in about two weeks.

The following were some of this section's highlights:

She observed stunning beaches, cliffs, and sunsets while riding along the Atlantic Ocean's shore.
- Crossing the Pyrenees, which had some difficult hills and descents
- Traveling through the Netherlands on a bicycle, where she liked the country's flat terrain and bike-friendliness - Visiting Paris, where she was inspired by the city's architecture and history - Getting to Berlin, where she passed the Brandenburg Gate and came to an end to her adventure

These were a few of the difficulties in this section:

- Having to deal with the cold and rain, which made her shiver and become wet.
- Locating adequate campsites or accommodations, which were hard to come by or costly
- Avoiding automobiles and trucks, which were swift and hazardous
- Dealing with the headwinds and crosswinds, which slowed her down and fatigued her

Jenny's trek across the globe was a remarkable display of tenacity, bravery, and tenacity. In 124 days, 10 hours, and 50 minutes, she rode 18,413 kilometers. By 19 days, she shattered the previous mark for female cyclists. She became the first woman to ride single and unassisted around the globe.

Jenny's trip across the globe was a fantastic adventure filled with challenges and discoveries. She visited some of the world's most stunning and interesting locations. She got to know some of the most fascinating and motivating individuals on the planet. She picked up some of the most priceless and profound teachings there are.

Jenny is on a once-in-a-lifetime tour across the globe.

CHAPTER FIVE

THE RETURN

On October 18, 2018, Jenny arrived back in Berlin, capping up her trip and completing her goal. That was a happy, relieved, and contented moment. It was a time for celebration, acknowledgment, and gratitude. That was a historic, difficult, and adventurous time.

By seven o'clock, Jenny arrived at the Brandenburg Gate. Lee Craigie and a few other Adventure Syndicate members welcomed her back and stood by her side. They congratulated her and offered her hugs and kisses. They also assisted her with parking her luggage and bike.

Jenny double-checked that her final time and distance had been recorded on her satellite tracker and smartphone. She looked at her watch to see the time as well. That was seven-ten. She'd completed it.

It had taken her 124 days, 10 hours, and 50 minutes to bike around the globe alone and without assistance. She has shaved 19 days off the previous record for female cyclists. She had broken the world record for the fastest female cyclist.

Jenny gave the camera that was recording her entrance a grin. Lee and the others who were supporting her waved back at her. She inhaled deeply and expressed gratitude to everyone.

She expressed her gratitude to her sponsors and backers for helping her with the logistics, finances, and equipment. She expressed her gratitude to her family and friends for their calls and words of support. She expressed her gratitude to her fans and followers for encouraging her via their comments and likes.

She praised herself for accepting the task and succeeding in it. She commended herself for her courage, her fortitude, and her resolve. She complimented herself for being inquisitive, daring, and receptive.

Jenny expressed her gratitude for the world serving as both her classroom and playground. She expressed her gratitude for the world's beauty, diversity, and amazingness. She expressed her gratitude for how difficult, unexpected, and gratifying the world was.

Jenny was surrounded by adoration, respect, and affection. She also felt a sense of appreciation, joy, and pride.

The voyage of a lifetime had just come to an end for her.

CONCLUSION

THE LESSONS

Not only was Jenny's voyage across the globe physically demanding, but it was also mentally and emotionally taxing. It was a voyage that included learning as well as travel. It was both an adventurous and a growth-oriented excursion.

Jenny's adventure taught her a lot of things. She gained knowledge about the world, herself, and other people. She gained knowledge about living, riding, and traveling.

We'll discuss some of the most significant lessons Jenny took away from her adventure in this chapter. We hope that these teachings will encourage and inspire you to take on new challenges and goals.

Lesson 1: You are more competent than you may believe.

Jenny discovered that she was stronger, tougher, and more resilient than she had previously believed. She discovered that she was capable of overcoming any challenge, issue, or setback that came her way. She discovered that she was capable of achieving any objective, hardship, or desire she set for herself.

Jenny discovered that she could cycle single and independently across the globe at record speed. She discovered that she was capable of remarkable things.

Jenny discovered that you are more competent than you believe. Everything you set your mind and heart to, you can do. You have the power to accomplish a remarkable feat.

Lesson 2: You are not traveling alone

Jenny discovered that she had more aid, friendship, and support than she had anticipated. She gained the ability to connect with people, seek their help, and depend on them. She discovered that she could inspire people, share her experience with them, and gain knowledge from them.

Jenny discovered that she was not traveling alone. She had sponsors, supporters, friends, family, and fans who assisted her with her budget, logistics, and equipment; who called and texted to cheer her on; and who left comments and liked her on social media.

Along the road, Jenny also encountered individuals who embraced her with warmth and generosity, shared their culture and knowledge with her, and became friends with her via their laughs and tales.

Jenny discovered that you are not traveling alone. You have individuals who look out for you, help you, and are with you. There are individuals in your life who inspire you, learn from you, and go with you.

Lesson 3: You are part of a larger planet.

Jenny discovered that she had more to see, experience, and learn than she had anticipated. She discovered that the world was more wonderful, diversified, and vast than she had previously realized. She discovered that there is a lot of wonder, beauty, and mystery in the world.

Jenny came to understand her place in a larger universe. She visited some of the world's most stunning and interesting locations. She got to know some of the most fascinating and motivating individuals on the planet. She learned some of the most important and priceless lessons ever.

Jenny discovered that everyone is part of a larger world. You have more to see, do, and learn than you would imagine. You have more to discover, value, and enjoy than you would imagine.

These are some of the lessons Jenny took away from her global travels. We anticipate that reading this book will teach you some of the concepts listed above.

We hope this book has educated and motivated you. We hope you have been inspired by and challenged by this book. We hope you have enjoyed and learned from this book.

We hope that this book has inspired you to go off on your global or local trip.

We hope that reading this book has inspired you to ride tenaciously.

Printed in Great Britain
by Amazon